TABLE OF CONTENTS

There is a glossary on page 30. Terms defined in the glossary are in type **that looks like this** on their first appearance.

WHAT IS HEAT?

Hello there!

I'm Heat!

I'm a form of energy that you experience every day!

Have you ever felt the warmth of the sun on your skin?

That sensation you feel...
That's me!

Have you ever sat around a fire?
Nice and toasty, right?

If you get too close, you might get burned.

But there's a lot more to me than that!

HOW DO WE USE HEAT?

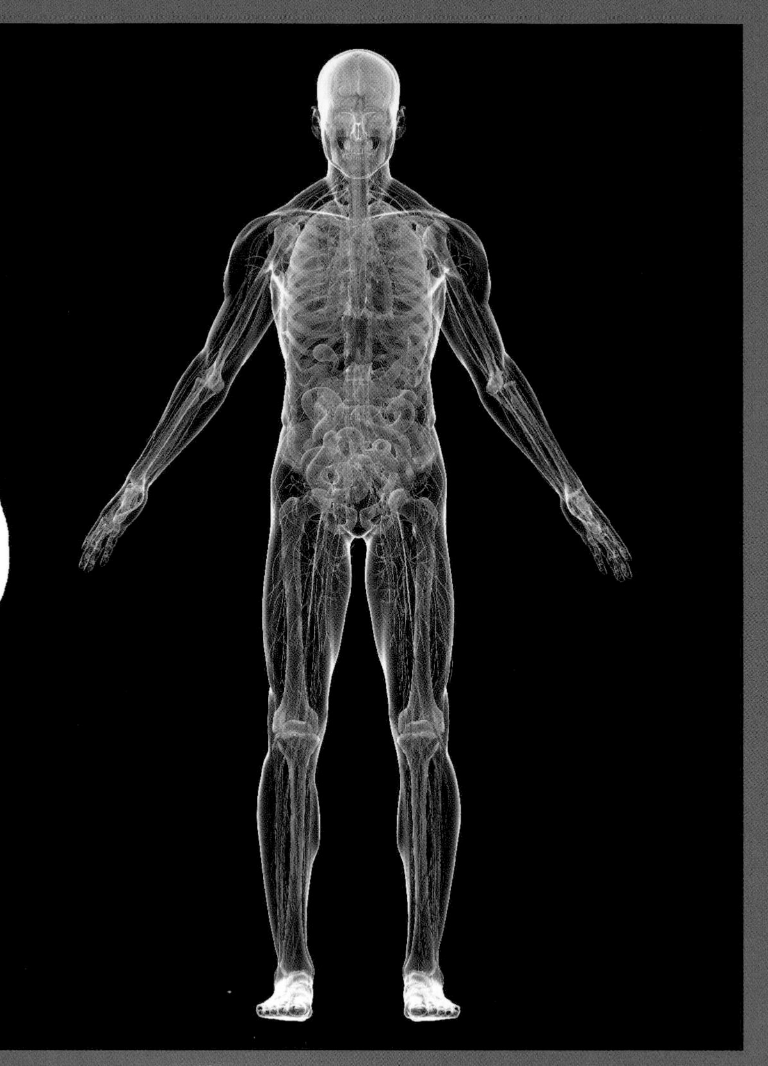

I'm an important part of your life. In fact, I'm inside your body right now.
Your body creates heat when it uses food.
That's how you maintain a steady temperature.

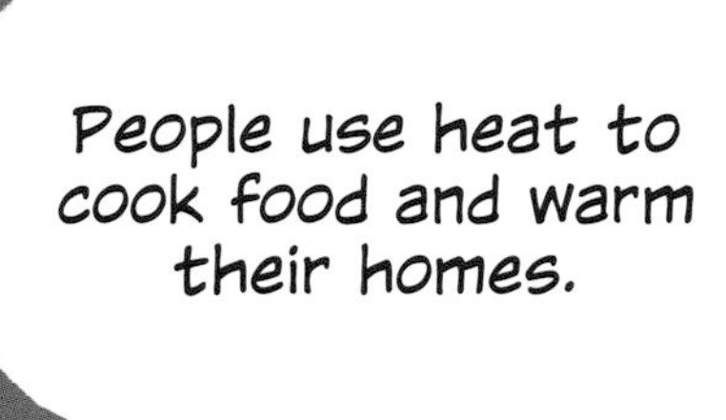
People use heat to cook food and warm their homes.

In factories, heat is used to bend and shape **metals!**

Iron melts at about 3000 degrees Fahrenheit (1535 degrees Celsius)!

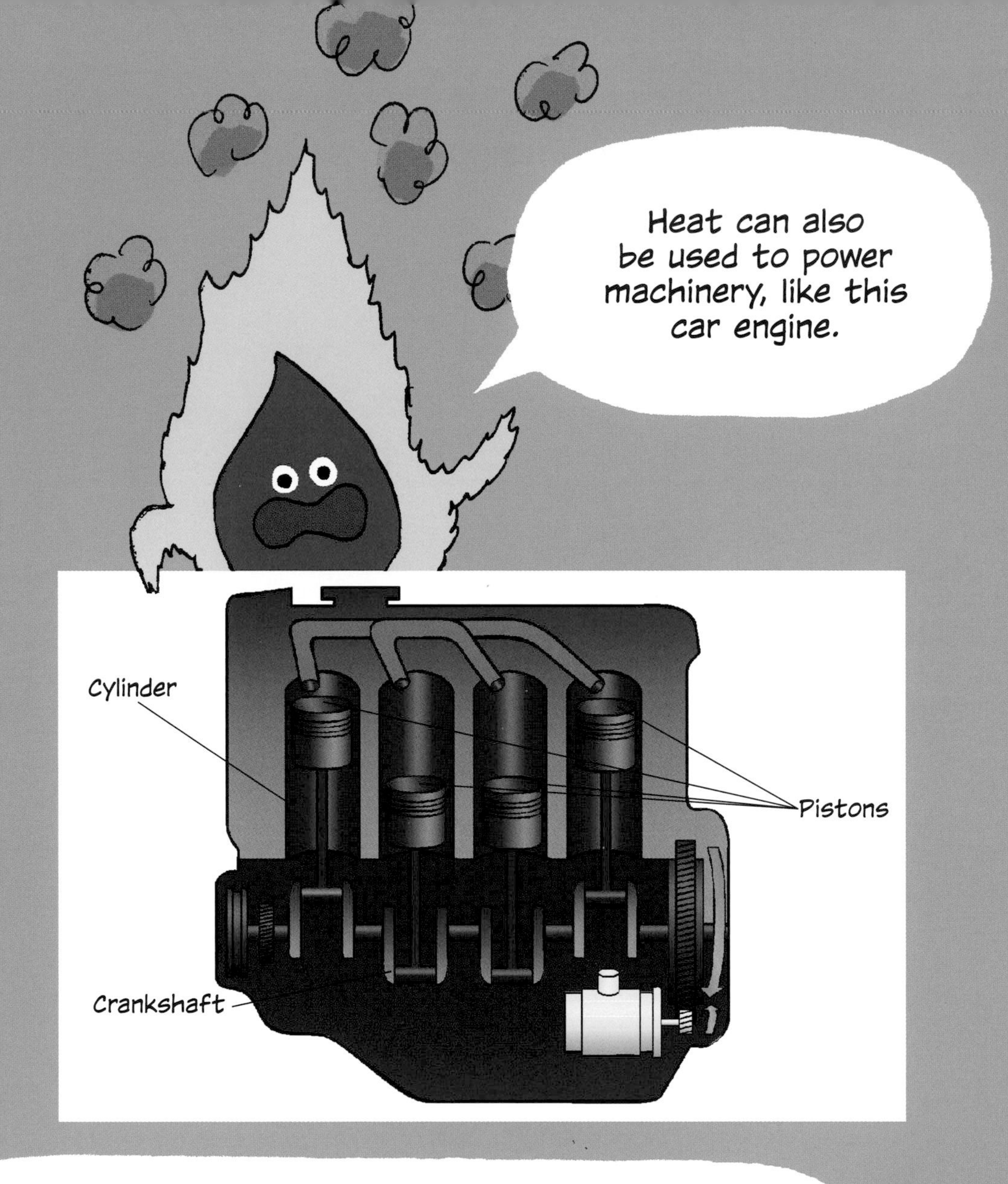
Heat can also be used to power machinery, like this car engine.
Cylinder
Pistons
Crankshaft

Did you know that the heat from burning fuels provides the power to move nearly all automobiles and airplanes?

Any machine that burns fuel uses heat.
Heat is even used to drive giant machines that make electric power.
Electric power runs everything from lights to toasters to computers.
So you see, heat is being used all around you!

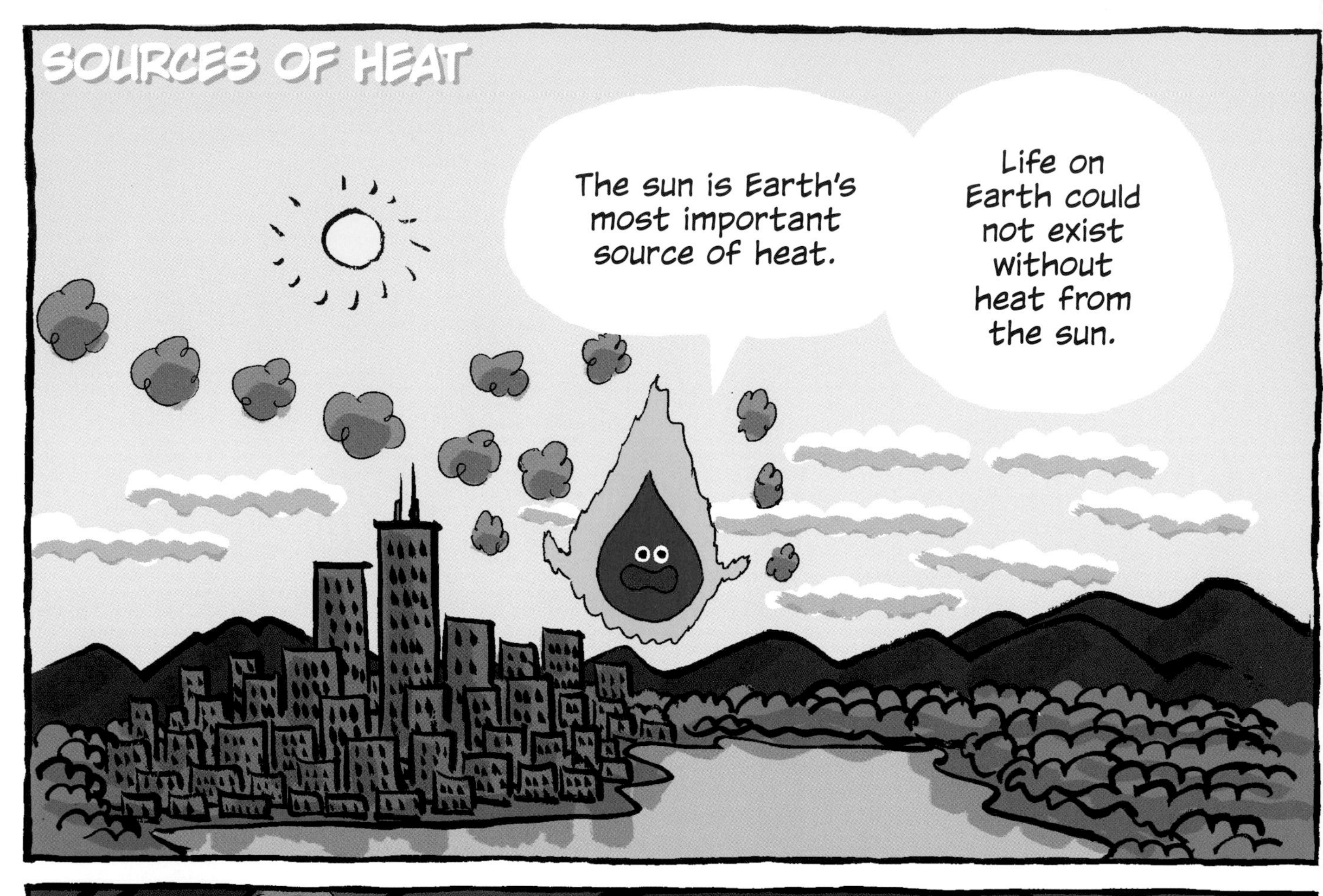
SOURCES OF HEAT
The sun is Earth's most important source of heat.
Life on Earth could not exist without heat from the sun.

Earth also has its own internal heat.
Earth is made up of layers of hot rock and metal.

Volcanoes, hot springs, and geysers all release heat from inside the planet.

Fires and electricity are other sources of heat.

You can also create heat by rubbing two objects together.

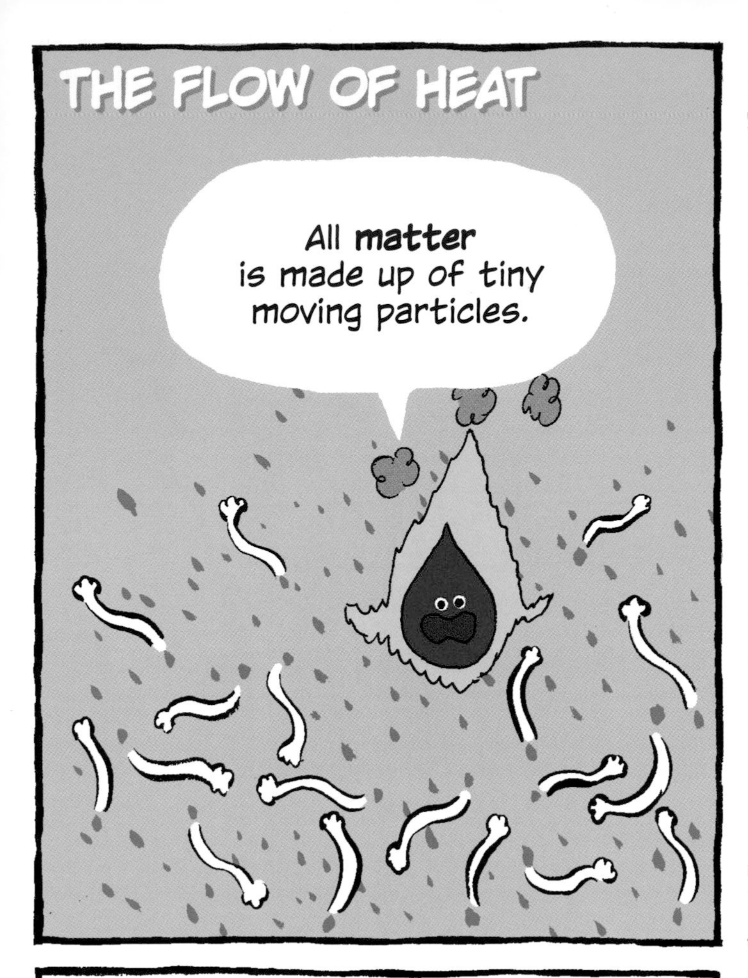
THE FLOW OF HEAT
All **matter** is made up of tiny moving particles.

The energy that makes them move is called **thermal energy.**
THERMAL ENERGY

When we heat matter, the thermal energy in its particles increases.
WOOF!

The more energy the particles have, the faster they move.
ZIP
ZIP
ZIP
ZIP
ZOOM

Thermal energy flows from particle to particle. It can also move between objects.
You can feel this flow of thermal energy as heat!
Boing
Boing
Boing
Particle
Particle
Particle

Hot objects have more thermal energy than cold objects.
HOT
COLD

Heat always flows from warmer objects to cooler objects.
Warm
cool

I *never* flow from cooler objects to warmer ones.

Let's look at how heat moves in a glass of ice water.
Boing
Boing
Boing

SPLASH
Boing

The particles in the ice are moving slowly.
The liquid water is warmer than the ice, so its particles are moving a little faster.

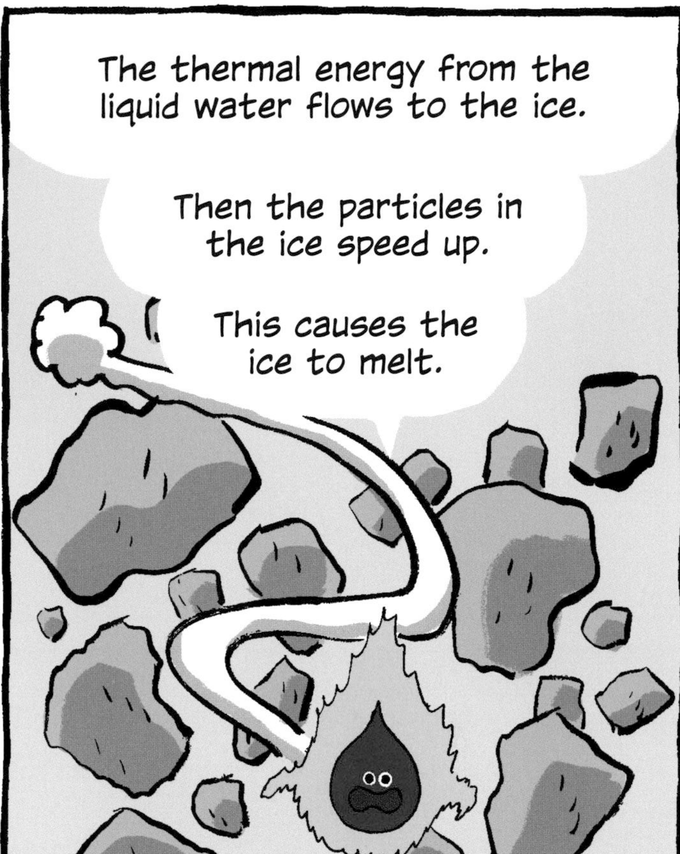
The thermal energy from the liquid water flows to the ice.
Then the particles in the ice speed up.
This causes the ice to melt.

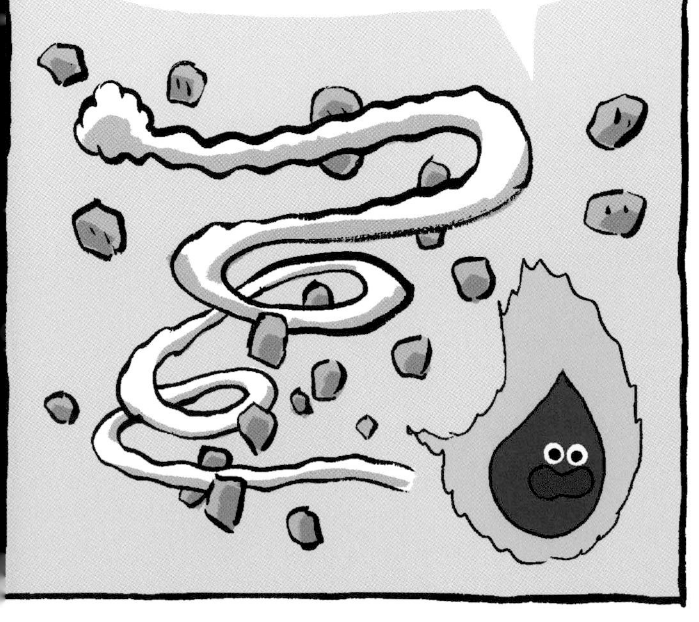
It changes from a solid to a liquid.
Eventually, all the water in the glass becomes the same temperature.

Now, all of the water particles in the glass are moving at the same **speed!**

EXPANSION AND CONTRACTION
Most solids and liquids **expand** when they are heated.
They get bigger.
This road is made of asphalt.
On a really hot day, the asphalt expands!
On a cold night, the particles of asphalt become smaller.
That's because most solids and liquids **contract** when they lose me!

smoosh
As the particles lose thermal energy, they move closer together.

This process of expansion and contraction causes the road to crack.

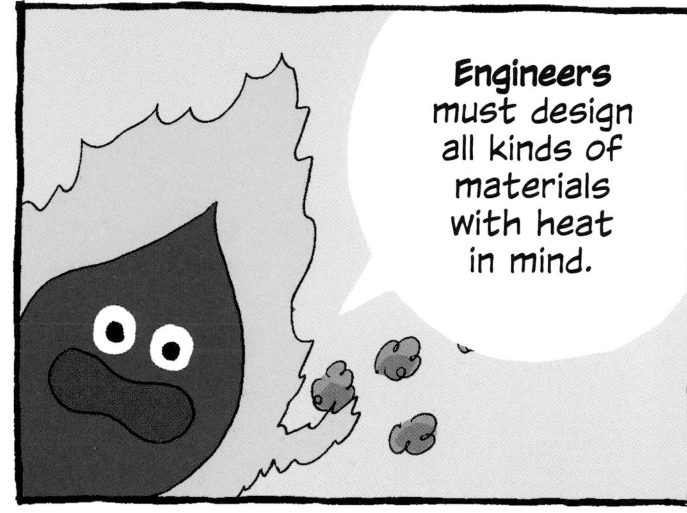
Engineers must design all kinds of materials with heat in mind.

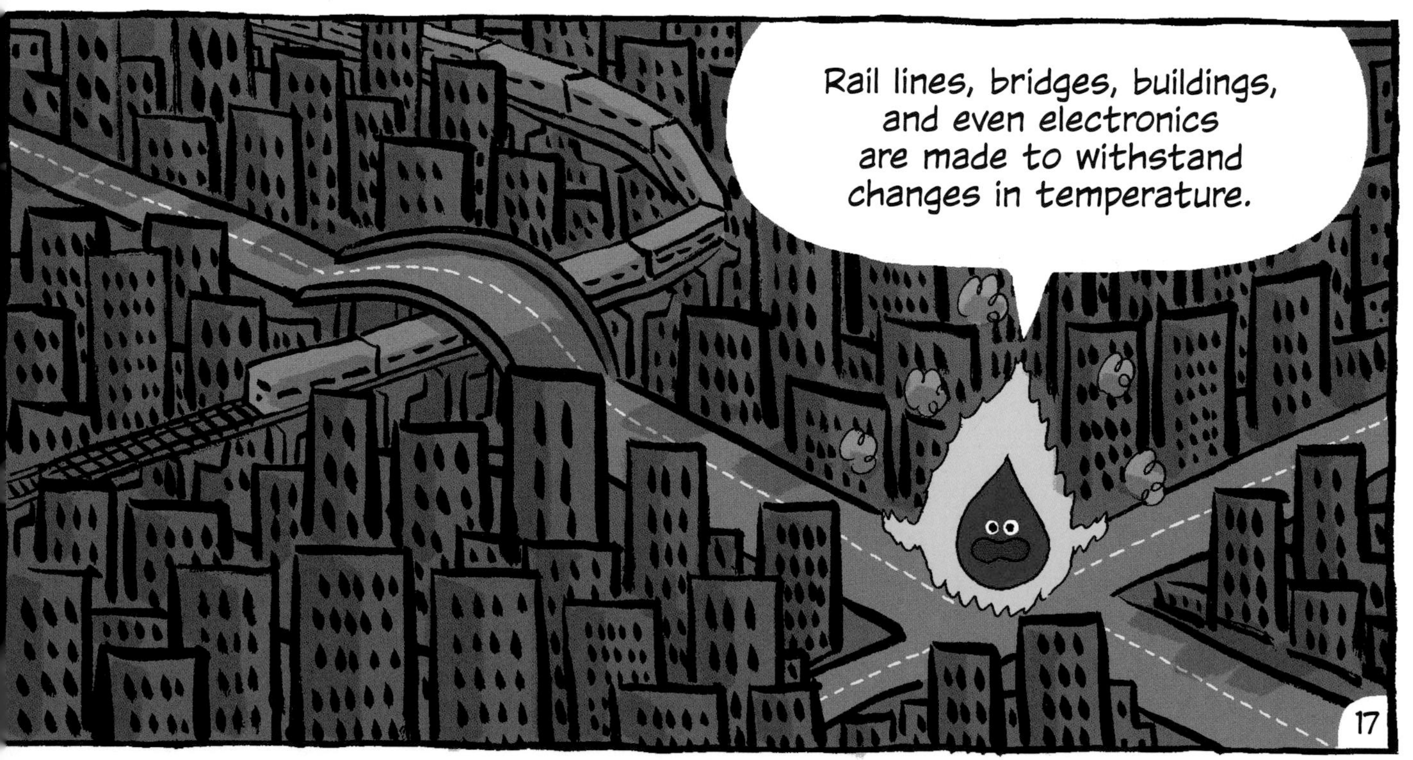
Rail lines, bridges, buildings, and even electronics are made to withstand changes in temperature.

Temperature is a measure of the thermal energy in an object.

Glass **thermometers** use expansion and contraction to measure temperature.

A glass thermometer is filled with a liquid.

When you measure the temperature of something hot, the liquid inside the tube gets heated. It expands and rises.

When you measure the temperature of something cold, the liquid contracts. It moves down the tube.

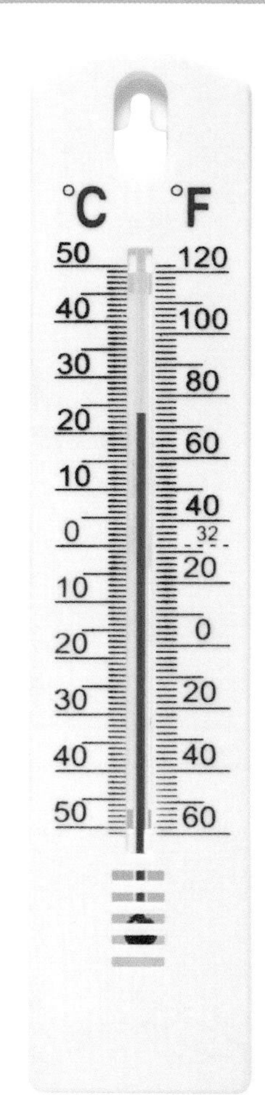

People use thermometers to measure temperature every day. How do you know what kind of clothes to wear?

You measure the temperature outside!

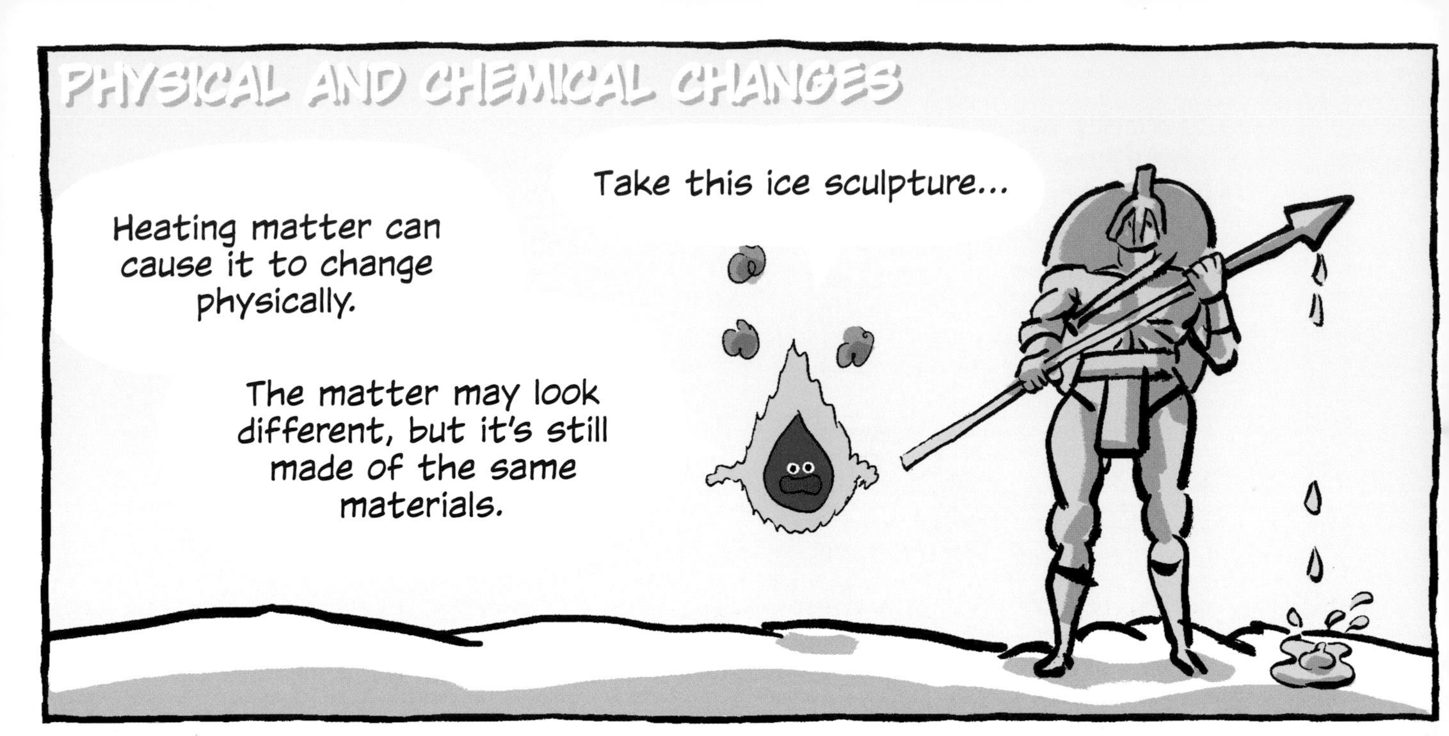
PHYSICAL AND CHEMICAL CHANGES
Heating matter can cause it to change physically.
The matter may look different, but it's still made of the same materials.
Take this ice sculpture...

When heat is applied to ice, it melts. It becomes liquid water.
PIP PIP PIP

And when the liquid water is heated, it changes into **water vapor,** a gas. It is still water, just in a different state.

Metals also melt if they are heated to high temperatures.
Sag

This is how we can shape and mold metals into objects.

Heat can also cause some kinds of materials to burn.
Burning is a sign of a **chemical change.**
The substances that make up the matter change into new substances.

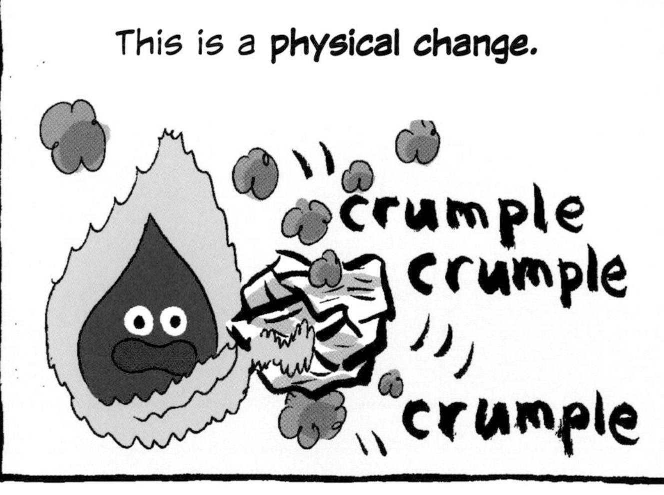
This is a **physical change.**
crumple
crumple
crumple

This is a chemical change.

As you can see, the paper isn't paper anymore. It has changed into something else.
Ash!

Whenever you produce a new substance, that's evidence of a chemical change.
WOOF

CONDUCTION

Heat is always on the move, but I don't always move the same way.

Sometimes I move from particle to particle, much like dominoes tipping over. This allows me to travel through a material.
TIP

The movement of heat from one particle to another is called **conduction.**
CONDUCTION

Solids are often heated by conduction. The particles in solids don't move around freely.
Thermal energy causes them to vibrate in place and bump into nearby particles.

If you leave a metal spoon in a hot pot of food, BEWARE!

The entire spoon will heat up!

The hot food heats up the tip of the spoon...

Then hot particles in the tip of the spoon shake faster and bump into the particles next to them. This transfers thermal energy.

These particles then bump into other particles.

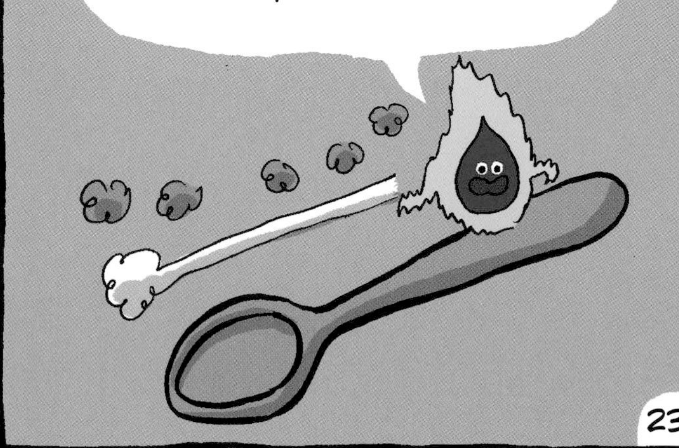
This is how heat moves up the spoon's handle.

CONVECTION AND RADIATION

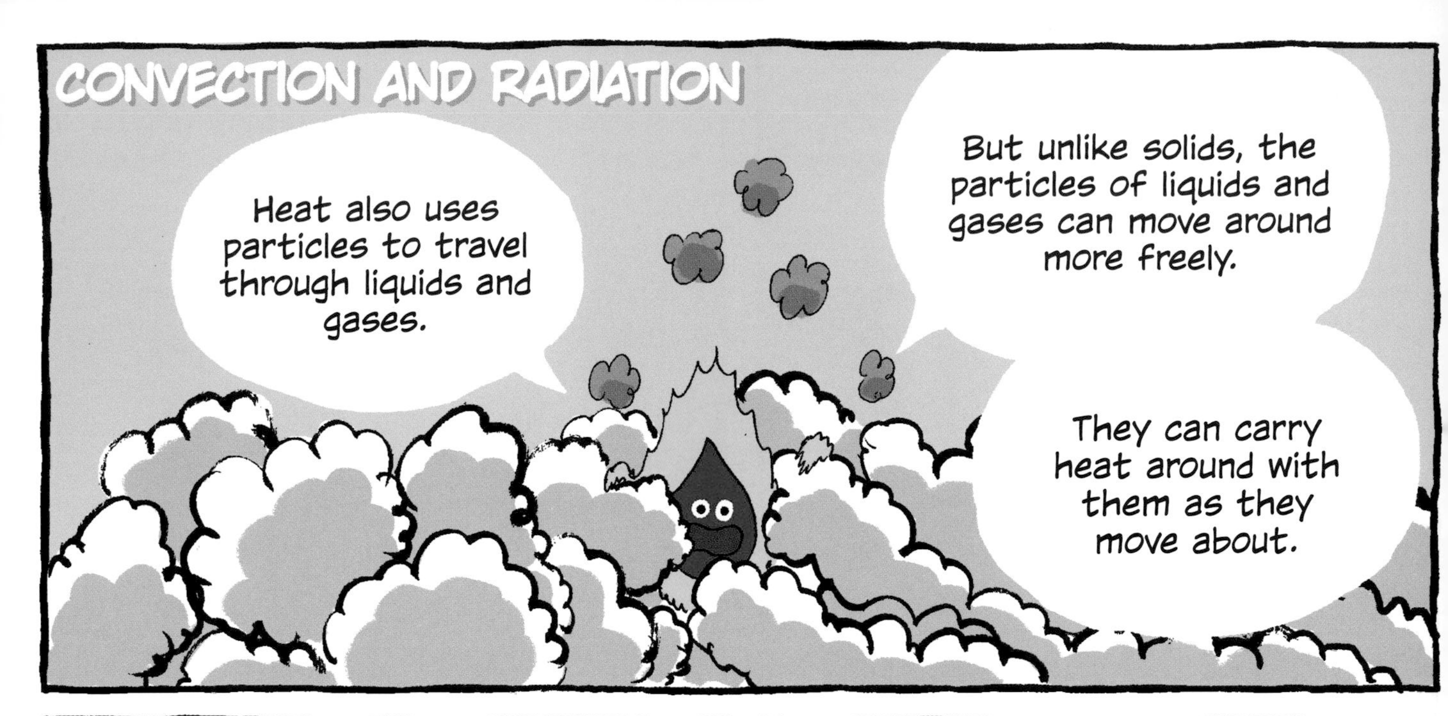

Heat also uses particles to travel through liquids and gases.
But unlike solids, the particles of liquids and gases can move around more freely.
They can carry heat around with them as they move about.

In a pot of boiling water, heated water at the bottom of the pot expands.

It rises to the top, forcing the cooler water to the bottom. Then the cooler water becomes warm and rises.

This movement of heat is called **convection.** Convection acts like a conveyor belt to move heat from one place to another.

Some kinds of heat can travel through empty space.
The movement of heat without any matter to carry it is called **radiation.**
RADIATION

Heat from the sun travels through space to warm Earth.

Heat can also be transferred by radiation where matter is present.
Sup?

You can feel the warmth of a nearby fire even if the air is still. Heat from the fire can travel to your skin by radiation.

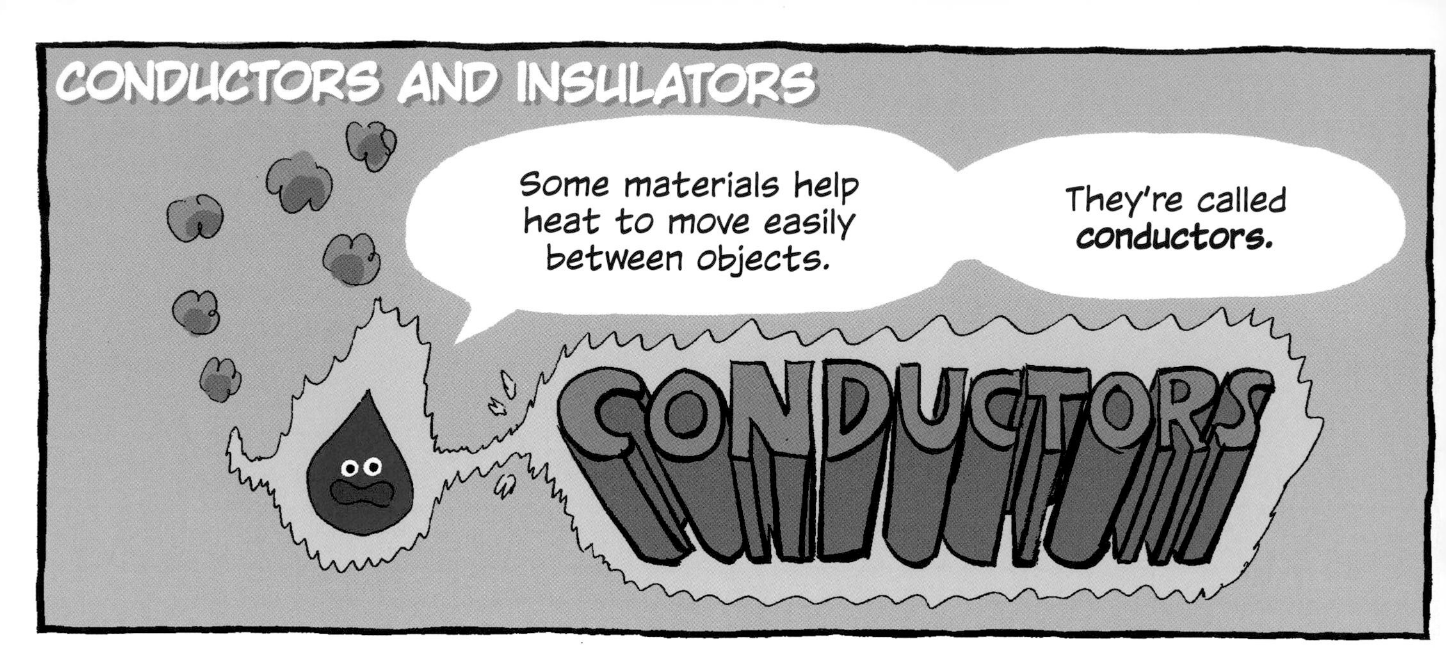

CONDUCTORS AND INSULATORS
Some materials help heat to move easily between objects.
They're called **conductors.**
CONDUCTORS

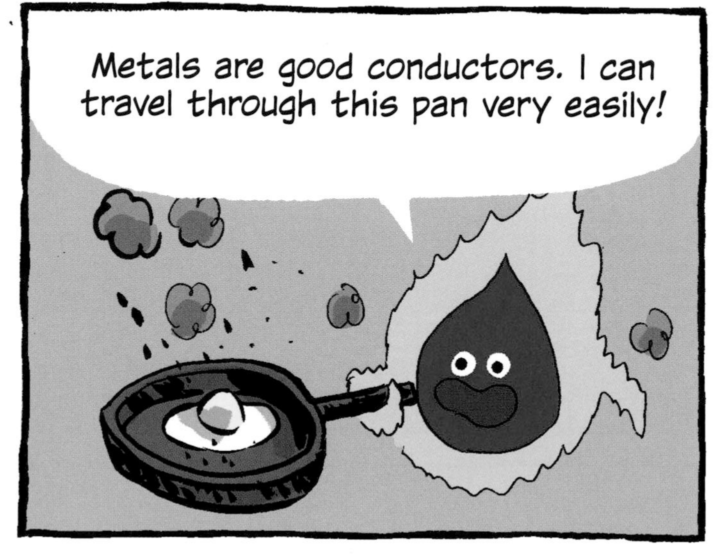

Metals are good conductors. I can travel through this pan very easily!

Insulators are materials that reduce the **motion** of heat.
INSULATORS

You need an insulator to touch a hot pan.

This oven mitt works great!

A winter jacket is another good insulator.

Winter jackets are made of materials like cotton, nylon, and down feathers.
These materials are insulators.
POOF

They do not conduct much heat away from your body.

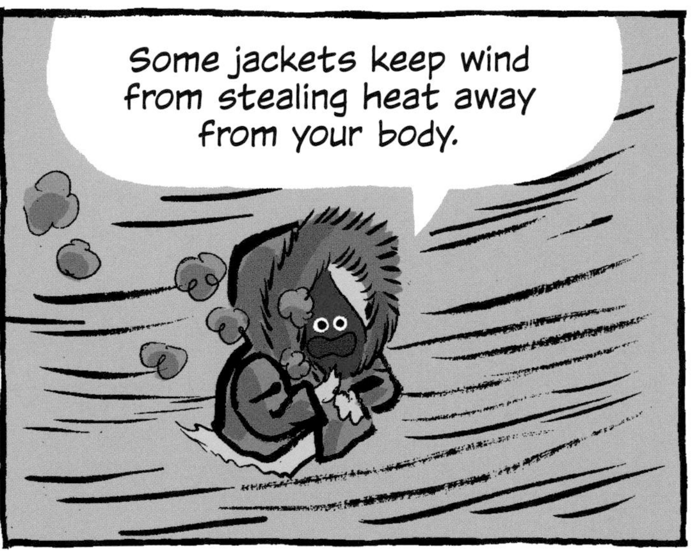
Some jackets keep wind from stealing heat away from your body.

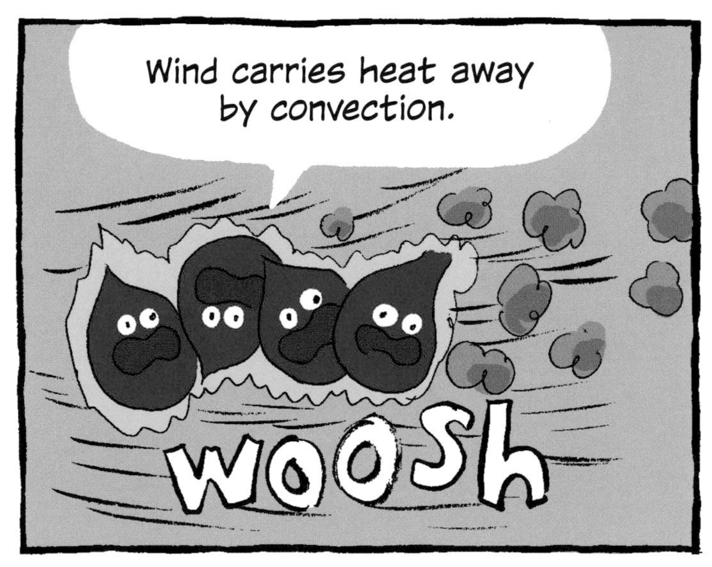
Wind carries heat away by convection.
WOOSH

Your home is like a big winter jacket.

Its walls are packed with insulation to keep heat in on cold days and out on hot days.

WHY STUDY HEAT?

Buildings and other structures would crumble to the ground if they were made with no account for different temperatures.

If your jacket were made of a conductor instead of an insulator, you'd freeze!
BRRR!
BRRR!

If this pot were made of an insulator instead of a conductor, the food would heat up very slowly!
If it were made out of wood, it would burn up!

As long as you're careful, you can use your new knowledge of heat to do amazing things!
What are you waiting for?!

GLOSSARY

chemical change a change in which one substance is converted into one or more substances with different properties.

conduction the movement of heat through a material.

conductor something that allows heat, electricity, light, sound, or another form of energy to pass through it.

contract to decrease in size.

convection the transfer of heat by the movement of gas or liquid.

engineer a person who plans and builds engines, machines, roads, bridges, canals, forts, or the like.

expand to increase in size.

insulator something that prevents the passage of electricity, heat, or sound.

matter what all things are made of.

metal any of a large group of elements that includes copper, gold, iron, lead, silver, tin, and other elements that share similar qualities.

motion a change in position.

physical change a change in which matter changes shape or form.

radiation energy given off as waves or small bits of matter. Heat from the sun is one example of radiation.

speed the distance traveled in a certain time.

thermal energy the force that makes particles of matter vibrate and move.

thermometer a tool for measuring temperature.

water vapor water in the state of a gas.

FIND OUT MORE

Books

All About Heat by Lisa Trumbauer (Children's Press, 2003)

Changing Materials by Chris Oxlade (Crabtree Publishing Company, 2008)

Conductors and Insulators by Angela Royston (Heinemann Library, 2008)

Energy: Heat, Light, and Fuel by Darlene R. Stille and Sheree Boyd (Picture Window Books, 2004)

Hot and Cold by Darlene R. Stille (Compass Point Books, 2001)

Sizzling Science Projects with Heat and Energy by Robert Gardner (Enslow Elementary, 2006)

Temperature by Navin Sullivan (Marshall Cavendish Benchmark, 2007)

Temperature: Heating Up and Cooling Down by Darlene R. Stille and Sheree Boyd (Picture Window Books, 2004)

Websites

Exploratorium: Science Snacks About Heat
http://www.exploratorium.edu/snacks/iconheat.html
Quick and easy experiments turn everyday objects into physics lessons at this website.

Infrared Zoo
http://coolcosmos.ipac.caltech.edu/image_galleries/ir_zoo/index.html
Remember, heat is inside many living things—including you! At this website, special cameras show you the heat differences between different kinds of animals.

Kids' Science Experiments: Heat
http://www.kids-science-experiments.com/cat_heat.html
Try some of these fun experiments to learn more about heat and how it works.

Physics4Kids: Thermodynamics and Heat
http://www.physics4kids.com/files/thermo_intro.html
This site offers an in-depth look at heat, heat transfer, and temperature.

Physics Central: Physics at Home
http://www.physicscentral.com/experiment/physicsathome/topic.cfm?q_topic=Thermodynamics%20%26%20Heat
These experiments in heat and thermodynamics will have you racing molecules and building your own thermometer.

Physics Life
http://www.physics.org/interact/physics-life/web/physics_life/
See how heat and other kinds of energy interact to make daily life possible at this interactive website.

Science Kids: Heat Quiz!
http://www.sciencekids.co.nz/quizzes/heat.html
Take this quiz and test your knowledge of heat and temperature.

Study Jams: Solids, Liquids, and Gases
http://teacher.scholastic.com/activities/studyjams/matter_states/
At this site, follow along with videos, karaoke, quizzes, and vocabulary exercises to learn about heat, particles, and states of matter.

INDEX